Influential Blogging for Beginners

Influential Blogging for Beginners

Hugh Richards

ISBN/SKU: 979-8-3303-7013-9

Published by Bald and Bonkers Network Academy, an imprint of Bald and Bonkers Network LLC.

Disclaimer

This book has been written for information purposes only. Every effort has been made to make this book as complete and accurate as possible. However, there may be mistakes in typography or content. Also, this book provides information only up to the publishing date. Therefore, this book should be used as a guide—not as the ultimate source. The purpose of this book is to educate. The author and the publisher do not warrant that the information contained in this book is fully complete and shall not be responsible for any errors or omissions. The author and publisher shall have neither liability nor responsibility to any person or entity with respect to any loss or damage caused or alleged to be caused directly or indirectly by this book.

CONTENTS

| VI | –

Introduction

If writing is an art form, then blogging is its own unique masterpiece. Bloggers are modern-day wordsmiths, carefully selecting phrases to capture their thoughts, emotions, dreams, and more.

Originally dubbed "weblogs" as they referred to server log files, blogs emerged in the mid-1990s and quickly transformed the internet into a treasure trove of information. While traditional web logging required a website and domain name, blogging simplified things—you only need an account with a blog provider, and often, these are free!

In the early days, blogs were personal journals where people shared their daily lives and thoughts. While not everyone aspired to fame, blogging became a platform for self-expression. As online businesses started to bloom, blogs evolved into powerful tools for promoting products and services, helping businesses enhance their online presence and drive sales.

Want to dive into the world of blogging, whether for fun or profit? Here are some tips to make your blog stand out:

Know Your Audience

Even if your blog is personal, it's important to think about your readers. Craft content that engages them. People blog not just for personal reasons but also to connect with others, so aim for clarity and accessibility in your writing.

Use Visuals

Add images to make your blog visually appealing. You don't need to include pictures of yourself—any relevant photos will do, as long as they are respectful and enhance your content.

Offer Value

While you have the freedom to write about anything, aim to create content that provides value. Whether it's informative or thought-provoking, your blog should offer something useful to your readers.

Keep It Simple

Avoid overly complex language and technical jargon. Most internet users skim rather than read word-for-word, so keep your posts concise and straightforward.

Encourage Interaction

Make your blog interactive by including multimedia like videos or audio clips. Consider adding a comments section to invite feedback and engage with your readers. You might even make new connections through your blog!

Blogs aren't just about having fun—they serve a purpose in the digital world. For those eager to hone their writing skills, blogging is a fantastic modern avenue for creative and commercial expression.

1

Beginners Guide To Blogging

A blog is essentially your digital diary, where you can jot down thoughts, ideas, and anything else you want to share with the world. Blogs come in a variety of styles and formats, tailored to fit the preferences of their creators. Many platforms offer features like hyperlinks, text, images, and even multimedia elements such as videos and audio clips.

Some bloggers opt for audio blogging, where they record spoken word entries instead of traditional text. Here's a quick rundown of key blog features:

- **Title**: Label your post.
- **Body**: The main content.
- **Trackback**: Link back to other sites.
- **Permanent Link**: Each post has its own URL.
- **Comments**: Allow readers to engage with your content.

One of the perks of blogging is its simplicity. Unlike multi-page websites, blogs use a few templates that make it easy to create new posts. This straightforward setup is perfect for beginners who want to start blogging right away.

Starting a blog is easy—just join a blogging platform, and you're part of a community where you can connect with other bloggers, share links, and comment on their posts. Blogs cover everything from personal journals to themes like sports, politics, and social commentary. They're also a great way for businesses to advertise, and for educators to share lesson materials.

For those interested in making money, blogs offer opportunities through advertising or promoting products. Many first-time bloggers use their blogs as personal journals to share daily experiences, thoughts, and creative works.

Blogging fosters a sense of community by allowing people to exchange ideas and feedback. To get started, browse blog directories to see what's out there and find a community that suits your interests. Most blogging sites are free, making it easy to dive in and get started.

Setting up a blog is straightforward and can be done for free through platforms like Blogger.com or WordPress.com. Both offer robust features, though WordPress is known for its advanced options. After setting up, play around with features like permalinks and trackbacks to familiarize yourself with the blogging world.

Get ready to explore, create, and potentially profit from your blog as we delve into strategies for monetizing your content and keeping readers engaged. Happy blogging!

2

Boosting Your Business With Blogging

A business blog is a powerhouse of online marketing that can save you thousands of dollars while opening up fantastic opportunities with just a single click. Blogs are user-friendly, customizable, and flexible, making them an excellent tool for showcasing your products and positioning them effectively in the market.

Here's why business blogging gives you a competitive edge:

Word-of-Mouth Power

With over 14 million blogs and 80,000 new ones popping up daily, blogging reaches a massive audience. About 30% of internet users are blog readers. Picture the impact of your product being featured in a blog—it can quickly spread through the internet, bringing your message to countless potential customers.

Building Awareness and Loyalty

Blogging allows for open communication with your audience, fostering trust and loyalty. Engaging with readers through comments and questions makes them more inclined to try your products and services.

Valuable Feedback

Blogs are a goldmine for product research and reviews. By observing customer feedback and behavioral patterns, you can refine your products and address concerns swiftly.

Community Influence

Bloggers are known for being friendly and supportive. They're eager to create discussions about your product. By actively participating in this blogging culture, your product will be top of mind for their next shopping trip.

To maximize your marketing impact, actively promote your business blog by submitting it to blog search sites and directories, and always include your URL. Ensure your blog is packed with valuable, exclusive information and is regularly updated to keep readers coming back for more.

Think of your blog as a booth at the world's biggest trade show—opportunities for marketing are just around the corner. Utilize Really Simple Syndication (RSS) feeds to enhance your blog's reach. Effective keyword usage will boost your search engine ranking, driving more traffic to your site and increasing potential sales.

Getting Started with Blogging

Blogging is a fantastic way to boost your marketing strategy, and setting up a blog is easy and often free. Here's how to get started:

1. **Choose Your Platform**: Start with free blogging platforms like Blogger.com or

WordPress.com. Both offer robust features, but WordPress provides advanced options like Trackbacks and Categories.

2. **Get Familiar**: Post your first entry, experiment with different templates, and explore the features.

3. **Understand Key Terms**:

- **Permalink**: The permanent URL for each blog post.
- **Trackback**: A way to link back to other blog posts (available on WordPress).
- **Pinging**: Notifies aggregators when your blog is updated, helping to drive traffic.

4.   **Design Your Blog**: Use pre-designed templates or, if you opt for a paid service, work with a designer to match your company's branding.

5.   **Pick Your Topics**: Choose topics that align with your business goals and test different ideas.

Blogging Best Practices:

- **Include Disclaimers**: Protect your business by outlining legal limits and disclaimers.
- **Create Blogging Policies**: Set clear guidelines on who can blog and what information can be shared.
- **Avoid Over-Promotion**: Keep your content engaging rather than overtly sales-focused.
- **Update Regularly**: Ensure your content is fresh and relevant.

- **Stay True to Core Values**: Reflect your company's values in your posts.
- **Encourage Employee Participation**: Get your team involved in blogging.

Start with 20 posts to establish your presence, then begin marketing. Regularly monitor reader engagement and adjust your strategy as needed. Consistency and relevance are key.

Why Blogging Rocks as an Internet Marketing Tool:

1. **It's Simple**: Anyone with basic internet skills can blog and share ideas.
2. **It's Authentic**: Blogs offer genuine insights and experiences, building trust with readers.
3. **It's Free**: Many blogging platforms offer free options, making it an affordable marketing tool.
4. **It Builds Credibility**: Consistent, valuable content establishes you as an industry expert.

5. **It Expands Your Market**: Use email, sub-scriptions, surveys, networks, and RSS feeds to grow your readership.

Embrace blogging as your go-to marketing tool and watch your business thrive!

Blog Content Brainstorming

Let's face it—keeping your blog fresh and engaging is essential for retaining your audience! Regular updates are key, and we're here to explore how you can keep those ideas flowing.

First things first: blog about what excites you. If you're passionate about your topic, your enthusiasm will shine through in your writing. No one wants to force themselves to write about something they're not interested in—it's like dragging your old job along with you. Write about what you love, and your readers will feel that energy.

Once you've picked your main theme, make posting a daily habit—even if it's just a quick comment on a recent news article. Think of your blog like a massive locomotive: it takes some effort to get started, but once you're rolling, you'll build unstoppable momentum.

Even the most knowledgeable bloggers can hit a wall, so here's how to keep those content ideas coming. Start by checking out what other bloggers in your field are talking about. Tools like Google Blog Search or Technorati can help you find relevant blogs. You can gather inspiration, and even engage with other bloggers through comments.

If you're still stuck, browse news articles related to your niche on sites like Google News or Yahoo News. Joining forums related to your topic can also spark new ideas. Pick a couple of forums with a large number of members or the most focus on your niche, and engage in conversations. This will build a treasure trove of questions, answers, and discussions to fuel your blog.

Consistency is key: aim to post at least once a day or more if you have ample content. Search engines love fresh content, and frequent updates will keep your blog on their radar, attracting more traffic. But don't worry—we'll dive deeper into traffic and SEO later. For now, keep that locomotive moving!

Blogging Basics

A blog is a dynamic website featuring articles that can include text, photos, videos, audio files, and hyperlinks. Blogs are typically presented in reverse chronological order and can serve various purposes:

- **Online Journal or Diary**: A personal space for daily thoughts or experiences.
- **Content Management System**: Organizes and manages content efficiently.
- **Online Publishing Platform**: A stage for publishing various content types.

Key Components of a Blog

- **Post Date**: When the entry was published.
- **Category**: The blog's topic or genre.
- **Title**: The heading of the blog post.
- **Main Body**: The content of the post.
- **RSS and Trackback**: Links to and from other blogs.
- **Comments**: Reader feedback.
- **Permalinks**: The URL of the full post.
- **Optional Items**: Calendar, archives, blogrolls, add-ons, or plug-ins.

Types of Blogs

- **Political Blog**: Covers news, politics, and activism.
- **Personal Blog**: An online diary of personal experiences and thoughts.
- **Topical Blog**: Focuses on a specific niche or local information.
- **Health Blog**: Discusses health issues, including medical news.
- **Literary Blog**: Also known as a litblog, focusing on literature.
- **Travel Blog**: Chronicles travel experiences.

- **Research Blog**: Academic and research-related content.
- **Legal Blog (Blawg)**: Covers legal topics and affairs.
- **Media Blog**: Critiques mass media inconsistencies.
- **Religious Blog**: Explores religious topics.
- **Educational Blog**: Educational content from students and teachers.
- **Collaborative Blog**: Written by multiple authors on a specific topic.
- **Directory Blog**: Lists various websites.
- **Business Blog**: Promotes businesses or discusses work-related topics.
- **Personification Blog**: Focuses on non-human entities or objects.
- **Spam Blog (Splog)**: Used for promoting affiliate sites.

Getting into Problogging

Problogging involves monetizing your blog. Here are some ways to make money:

- **Advertising Programs**: Place ads on your blog.
- **RSS Advertising**: Earn from RSS feeds.
- **Sponsorship**: Partner with brands for sponsored content.
- **Affiliate Programs**: Promote products for commissions.
- **Digital Assets**: Sell digital products.
- **Blog Network Writing**: Write for blog networks.
- **Consulting and Speaking**: Offer expertise and give talks.

Tips for Success in Problogging

- **Be Patient**: Building a profitable blog takes time.
- **Know Your Audience**: Target a specific group.
- **Be an Expert**: Focus on a niche and become the go-to source.
- **Diversify**: Experiment with various monetization strategies.

- **Engage Readers**: Create a welcoming, readable blog layout.

With the right approach, dedication, and enthusiasm, turning your blog into a profitable venture is entirely possible. Keep pushing forward, and remember: consistency and passion are your best allies!

4 |

The Importance Of Blog Design

B logs have skyrocketed in popularity over the years, becoming a go-to platform for both personal expression and professional communication. From individuals sharing their thoughts and feelings to companies updating consumers on the latest product news and reviews, blogging has become a key player in internet marketing.

In the past, online marketing mainly involved placing banners and links on popular news and information websites or in newsletters. Today, blogs are taking the spotlight. People now spend significant time reading blogs—whether from friends, favorite authors, or on topics of interest. As blogging grows, it's even starting to rival traditional news sources in popularity.

While blogs might not always be the most reliable for breaking news, they often provide trustworthy product reviews. Unlike media reviews influenced by sponsorships, blog writers share genuine experiences with products and services.

With the rise in blog traffic, there's a fantastic opportunity for product marketing. More traffic can translate into increased sales. To boost your blog's visibility, consider joining affiliate programs or getting your blog listed on popular sites. Just be mindful—this might cost a bit if you're new to blogging.

For newcomers eager to boost blog traffic, focus on delivering engaging and valuable content, and ensure your blog's design is appealing. Here are some tips to help your blog stand out:

1. **Customize Your Banner**: Upgrade from generic designs with a custom graphic that features your blog's title. You can either create your own or buy a professional-looking graphic online for a reasonable price.

2. **Personalize Photos**: Make your photos pop by adding borders or customizing them to match your blog's theme. This small touch can enhance the overall look and feel of your blog.

3. **Add a Favicon**: Favicons (the tiny icons that appear next to the URL in browsers) add a polished touch. These are easy to create with graphic editing software.

4.   **Include RSS Feeds**: RSS feeds let readers stay updated on your latest posts. There are plenty of tutorials online to help you set this up.

5.   **Incorporate Audio**: Adding audio elements like streaming radio or playlists can make your blog more engaging and keep visitors coming back for more.

6.   **Strategic Advertising**: If you're using Google Adsense, place ads thoughtfully so they don't disrupt the reading experience.

By implementing these strategies, you'll increase and retain blog traffic more effectively.

Understanding Blog Hosts

As blogs have evolved, so have the hosting services that support them. Whether it's for personal journals or business blogs, choosing the right host is crucial. Here's what to consider:

1. Hosting Options:

- **Self-Hosted**: Manage your own blog service.
- **Paid Hosting**: Opt for professional hosting to access advanced features.
- **Aggregator Pages**: Let employees select their own hosting if you prefer a decentralized approach.

2. Essential Features:

- **Comments**: Foster dialogue and gather customer feedback.
- **Trackback**: Enhance visibility and ease of access to your blog.
- **Categories and Tags**: Organize content for better navigation and searchability.
- **RSS Feed**: Share updates with readers efficiently.

3. Free vs. Paid Services: Free services are great for personal use, but paid options provide the features needed for effective business blogging, such as advanced analytics and support.

4. Choosing a Host: Look at other blogs hosted on potential platforms, check their layout and design, and ensure reliable technical support.

5. Blog Design and Management:

- **Create a Style**: Match the design to your audience's needs.
- **Tone**: Keep it open and credible.
- **Update Regularly**: Aim for frequent updates, ideally a few times a week.
- **Include Links**: Link to relevant sites and blogs.
- **Engage**: Write in a conversational, first-person tone.

Remember, your blog is a reflection of you and your company. Make it engaging, authentic, and reflective of your brand's personality. Happy blogging!

Blogging for Profit Begins With a Long Term Plan

Essential oils are therapeutic-grade extracts from various plants, offering a natural touch to wellness. Many people dream of making money through blogging, and it's a goal that's within reach with some effort and a basic understanding of blogging tools. However, achieving profit from a blog is tougher than it seems.

The main hurdles? Unrealistic expectations and lack of planning. Bloggers often expect rapid growth and substantial earnings, but when those goals aren't met, motivation can wane. Success requires a realistic plan and a big readership. The more visitors you attract, the more appealing your blog is to advertisers.

A common pitfall is focusing solely on writing without dedicating time to marketing. While frequent updates keep your blog relevant, it's crucial to invest effort in drawing visitors. Network with other bloggers, set up link exchanges, and explore proven traffic-boosting strategies.

Remember, building a profitable blog takes time—several months, at least. Set achievable goals, stay motivated, and reward yourself for hitting milestones.

Monetizing Your Blog

There are two main ways to profit from blogging:

1. **Advertising**: Sell ad space to companies or use programs like Google AdSense. AdSense is easy but often less lucrative. Direct

sales to companies can be more rewarding if you have industry contacts and a strong sales background.

2.   **Brand Promotion**: Create a blog that enhances a brand's image by forging positive consumer associations. This can be quite profitable if you have a knack for marketing.

If you already have an established blog, monetizing through ads could be just a step away. Sponsored links or banners can turn your blogging hobby into income. Even if your initial goal wasn't profit, you might find it easier than expected to earn some extra cash.

Ultimately, the profitability of your blog depends on its topic and audience. Blogs that attract desirable demographics for advertisers have the potential for higher earnings. So, if you're already blogging, consider exploring ads—you might be pleasantly surprised by the results.

6 |

Monetizing Your Blog

You've been putting in the hard work, crafting high-quality, original content, and your blog is seeing a solid stream of visitors. But let's be real—traffic alone isn't going to magically turn into cash. It's time to convert those clicks into coins!

Here's where monetization comes into play. One of the easiest ways to start earning from your blog is through Google AdSense. Head over to their website to dive into their advertising program. Let me share a few tips to make it work like a charm.

Google AdSense is a fantastic tool because when your readers finish with your latest post, they might be ready to leave your blog. If your AdSense ads are visible, they could click on something relevant and—cha-ching!—you've just made your first virtual cents. But remember, you won't be rolling in the dough if you don't optimize your ads. Make sure to place them strategically and blend them into your site's design so they look more like helpful links rather than flashy ads. Customize the color of your ad text and links to match your blog's style. If your blog uses black text with red links, make your ads follow suit!

Another great way to earn is through affiliate marketing. Recommend products to your readers and earn a commission when they make a purchase through your links. Let's say you're running a tech blog and discover Gadget X on a merchant's site that offers an affiliate program. Write a detailed review of Gadget X, highlighting its pros and cons, and include a link for your readers to buy it. If they click through and purchase, you'll earn a commission. Picture this: if just 1 out of every 100 visitors buys Gadget X, and you earn $27 per sale, 10,000 visitors could mean a $2,700 paycheck just for sharing one product!

Finding affiliate programs that fit your blog's theme is a breeze. Just search Google for "[Your Niche] + affiliate program" to discover opportunities that match your content.

More Monetization Options

We've covered AdSense and affiliate marketing, but there are more ways to cash in on your blog. Let's explore some additional options.

First up, check out **Chitika** (www.chitika.com). This innovative ad program serves highly relevant ads with detailed tabs like "Best Deals," "Details," and "Reviews," making the ads feel more like useful information than traditional promotions. This often leads to higher click-through rates.

Another option is becoming an affiliate for **Amazon.com**. Amazon offers a vast range of products, especially books, which can be perfect for any niche. Once you join, you can earn up to 7% commission by referring visitors. Use Amazon's templates to highlight recent items, feature specific deals, or weave referral links directly into your blog posts.

Lastly, if your blog is attracting a large audience, consider selling advertising space directly. Popular blogs can command prices starting at $150 per month for ad space, depending on traffic levels. Use tools like StatCounter (statcounter.com) to track your pageviews and visitors, and set up a detailed tracking system to manage your ad sales.

Even if your blog's traffic isn't massive yet, you can still sell ad space on a per-click or per-impression basis. Sites like AdBrite (adbrite.com) can help you get started.

With these strategies, you'll be well on your way to turning your blog into a profitable venture. Keep experimenting and optimizing, and watch those earnings grow!

Video Blogging

Getting Started with Video Blogging
Welcome to the exciting world of video blogging—the next frontier of online expression! While text blogs have long been the standard, video blogging takes storytelling and product showcasing to a whole new level. It's like giving your audience a front-row seat to your content with a live-action twist!

Video blogging, or vlogging, offers a dynamic way to connect with your audience. It might require a bit more technical know-how, like larger disk spaces, faster servers, and specialized software, but the rewards are well worth it. Think of it as turning your blog into a high-definition commercial—showcasing your products or services in all their glory.

Why Video Blogging Works Wonders

People are visual creatures, and nothing grabs attention quite like video. Just like a captivating TV commercial, a well-made video blog can showcase your product in action, leaving viewers not just interested but eager to buy. If you present your product effectively, it's almost like magic—people might just find themselves wanting something they never knew they needed!

On the web, where everything is often static, adding movement with video can make your content pop. Imagine your product strutting its stuff in a vibrant video blog—it's bound to catch eyes and generate buzz.

Getting Started with Your Home Studio

Starting a video blog doesn't mean you need a Hollywood budget. With just a web camera, microphone, video software, and good lighting, you can create engaging content right from your living room.

1.   **Invest in Quality Equipment**: A high-resolution web camera will ensure your video looks sharp and professional. Your viewers will appreciate the clarity, and your product will shine.

2.   **Illuminate Like a Pro**: Proper lighting is key to crisp, clear images. Make sure your filming area is well-lit, and don't shy away from using lighting effects to add some flair.

3.   **Sound Matters**: A good microphone is crucial for clear audio. Whether you're adding a voice-over or background music, ensure your sound enhances the video rather than distracting from it.

4.   **Edit with Ease**: Choose video editing software that suits your level of expertise. Even basic programs can help you polish your video, trim out bad angles, and integrate still images if needed. Select a background that complements your lighting for a seamless look.

Consider the Challenges

While video blogging is fantastic, it does have its challenges. It can slow down computers and may take longer to download, especially for those on slower connections. But don't let this deter you! Combine video with text and images to ensure your content is accessible to everyone.

Embrace Creativity and Interactivity

In today's competitive market, creativity is your best ally. Video blogging not only lets you showcase your products interactively but also draws viewers into your world. By engaging your audience and highlighting the benefits of your products, you're setting the stage for successful sales.

So gear up, get creative, and let video blogging help you captivate your audience and boost your business!

Conclusion

As we wrap things up, let's clear something up: there's no one-size-fits-all when it comes to the scope of your blog. The beauty of blogging is that you have the freedom to dive into whatever fascinates you. But here's the twist: the real difference between a blog that's raking in the cash and one that's just treading water lies in how you present it. Think about it—would you rather read your university professor's dense lecture notes or lose yourself in the latest page-turner from your favorite author?

Chances are, you'd gravitate towards the novel. It's engaging, lively, and way more enjoyable than a dry lecture. People generally prefer their reading material to be light and engaging. When folks visit your blog, they're not just hunting for information; they're looking for it to be served up in an easy, enjoyable way.

To draw in more visitors and keep them coming back for seconds, your blog needs a personal touch.

Imagine you're chatting with a close friend about a topic. Infuse your writing with a friendly tone, and if it fits, sprinkle in a bit of humor. After all, who doesn't enjoy a good laugh?

Another crucial point is to avoid talking to your readers as if you're delivering a formal speech. Write as though you're having a one-on-one conversation. This approach makes your readers feel like they're connecting with a friend, rather than being lectured by an authority figure.

Additionally, let your personality shine through your writing. Readers are naturally curious about the person behind the blog, and a unique voice can set you apart from the crowd. This isn't just about being memorable; it's about creating a brand that sticks. Just as people instantly think of McDonald's when they crave fast food or Nike when they need sports gear, your distinctive personality will make your blog the go-to source for your niche.

So, the takeaway is simple: write as if you're conversing with a single friend, not an audience.

Inject your own personality into your posts and make your blog a reflection of who you are. With these strategies, you'll not only attract readers but also turn them into loyal followers.